Lacé®
cutting and folding

Gerda Perik

FORTE UITGEVERS

Contents

Fourth edition June 2002
ISBN 90 5877 101 6

This is a publication from
Forte Uitgevers bv
Boothstraat 1c
3512 BT Utrecht
The Netherlands

For more information about the
creative books available from Forte
Uitgevers: www.hobby-party.com

Publisher: Marianne Perlot
Final editing: Hanny Vlaar
Photography and digital image
editing: Fotografie Gerhard Witteveen,
Apeldoorn, The Netherlands
Cover and inner design:
Studio Herman Bade BV, Baarn,
The Netherlands
Translation: TextCase, Groningen

Foreword

A new technique deserves to have a new name. The name chosen is the French word Lacé, which means to lace together.

The technique involves making a pattern of cuts and folding the loose edges over and under each other. The best effects are achieved by using duo-colour paper, where the front and rear have different colours.

I enjoyed sticking 3D pictures inside the circle. Adding a sticker or some text makes the card complete.

Festive cards are made using duo-colour papers with a gold or silver mother-of-pearl gloss.

Good luck,

Gerda

I dedicate this book to our first grandchild, Merel, who was born on 23rd May 2001.

Special thanks to
Our daughter Mariëlle for writing the text. Bert Siezen for designing the templates.
Marianne Perlot for making it possible to try the new Lacé templates.

Techniques

1. Cutting the Lacé border

The pattern to be cut out is shown on the light-green Lacé templates. Preferably use duo-colour paper with or without a mother-of-pearl gloss (or simply stick origami or holographic paper onto standard card).
Stick the template in the correct place on the card using non-permanent adhesive tape (or a paper plaster). If necessary, push the sticky side onto your clothing to reduce the stickiness.
Use the Lacé knife to cut through the openings. Start at the point and cut towards the side. Always use a knife with a sharp point.
Once you have cut all the lines, carefully remove the template and the adhesive tape from the card. Fold over every other shape which has been cut out and fold them under the points of the ones you do not fold over. You will now be able to see the other side of the duo-colour paper.

2. Copying the punch pattern

Photocopy the punch pattern in this book. Cut it out close to the outside edge or cut it out using a circle cutter. Stick the pattern onto the card using a small amount of photograph glue and punch out the design.

3. Punched circle edges

The following is very important when punching out a pattern:
- Hold the punch upside down so that you can see the opening of the punch.
- Place the opening over the design of the pattern.
- Punch out the entire design.
- Do not forget to remove the corners from the corner punches.

4. Making your own punch pattern

Determine the width of the punch design and multiply this by the number of designs you wish to use in your pattern to give you the circumference of the circle where the design will be located. Divide this number by π (pi=3.14) to find the diameter of the circle. Draw lines on the circle to help indicate the width of the designs. Use these lines to punch out the design. This involves quite a bit of calculation, so try it first on a piece of scrap card. It will be worth the extra effort.

5. 3D cut-outs

Cut out the pictures according to the instructions. Look carefully at what has been omitted in each layer. Fill the syringe with 3D glue. A nozzle

1. Duo-colour paper in many different colours.

2. Use the Lacé templates and the knife.

3. Cut out the pattern and lace this together.

4. Finish the card off.

which can be screwed onto the tube is included with the 3D glue. When you have finished, close the tube with the cap and leave the nozzle to dry. Use a cocktail stick to place small drops of 3D glue onto the entire back of the first picture. Place the picture onto the card using a pair of tweezers and carefully push it into place with the edge of the tweezers or a cocktail stick. Do not push it too hard, otherwise you will loose the necessary distance. Next, stick the other pictures on in the same way, one-by-one. Make sure each picture is directly above the others. This can be checked by holding the card at eye level. Once all the layers have been stuck on, allow the card to dry for two hours.

Tip: Stick origami paper onto single-sided sticky film first and then cut the pattern out using the circle cutter.

Materials

- ❏ Duo-colour paper (with or without mother-of-pearl gloss)
- ❏ Lacé templates (by Kars)
- ❏ No. 1 Rectangle, large angle
- ❏ No. 2 Rectangle large/small angle
- ❏ No. 3 Round, leaf point
- ❏ No. 4 Round, round angle
- ❏ No. 5 Round, tooth
- ❏ No. 6 Round, fan arch
- ❏ No. 7 Round, large angle
- ❏ No. 8 Round, large/small angle

- ❏ 3D Scratch and Smell sunflower sheet (by Kars)
- ❏ 3D cut-out sheets
- ❏ Shake-it cut-out sheets
- ❏ Adhesive pictures of butterflies (by Kars)
- ❏ Squirrel poster sheet
- ❏ Adhesive stars
- ❏ Embossing stencils EC9722 and EC 9725 (by Avec) (for text)
- ❏ Gel pens
- ❏ Ornare pricker and prick mat
- ❏ Beads

- ❏ Embroidery needle and thread
- ❏ Adhesive tape
- ❏ Photo glue
- ❏ 3D glue/silicon glue
- ❏ Scissors
- ❏ Cutting mat
- ❏ Knife
- ❏ Punches
- ❏ String
- ❏ Ribbon
- ❏ Double-sided adhesive tape
- ❏ Eyelet and eyelet punch

Card page 1

What you need:
- ❏ *Lacé template no. 6*
- ❏ *Card: Yellow no. 400 and red no. 505 (by Canson Mi-Teintes)*
- ❏ *Ornare cut-out sheets: OK 023 (Congratulations) and OK 026 (Get well soon)*
- ❏ *Embossing stencil EC 9722 (by Avec)*
- ❏ *Red and yellow gel pens*
- ❏ *Blue origami paper*

Double red and yellow cards (14 x 14 cm). Blue origami paper (13 x 13 cm). Yellow/red duo-colour paper (12.5 x 12.5 cm).
Stick the pictures onto the card using 3D glue.

Draw decorative lines and write appropriate text using the embossing stencil.

Card page 3

What you need:
- ❏ *Lacé template no. 6*
- ❏ *Distance flower punch*
- ❏ *Green gel pen*
- ❏ *Shake-it cut-out sheet IT 329*

Yellow/green duo-colour paper (10.5 x 10.5 cm).
Stick the violet onto the card using 3D glue. Draw a green decorative line around the card 0.5 cm from the edge. Punch out flowers and stick them in the corners.

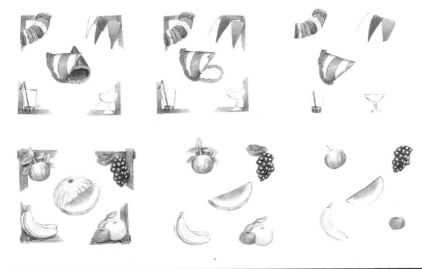

Spring

Fresh colours and

sunny flowers.

What you need:
- ❏ *Blue/yellow duo-colour paper*
- ❏ *Lacé templates no. 1 and 3*
- ❏ *3D Scratch and Smell sunflower sheet (by Kars)*
- ❏ *Shake-it cut-out sheets: IT 329 and IT 330 (violets)*
- ❏ *Blue and yellow gel pens*
- ❏ *Ornare pricker and prick mat*
- ❏ *2 mm beads (by Rayher)*
- ❏ *Silver origami paper*

Make the Lacé border as described in Techniques.

Matching envelopes can be made as shown by the diagrams on page 31.

1. and 2. Square cards
Double card (10 x 10 cm). Lacé template no. 3.
Prick holes in all the corners of the Lacé pattern
and use them to sew yellow or lilac beads onto

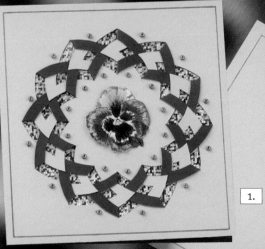

1.

3.

2.

the pattern. Stick silver origami paper (9.8 x 9.8 cm) against the inside. Stick a piece of duo-colour paper the same colour as the card over this to make it look nice. Use a gel pen to draw a decorative line around the card 0.5 cm from the edge. Curl the edges of the violet to give a raised effect and stick to card with 3D glue.

3. and 4. Rectangular card
Double card (14.8 x 10.5 cm). Lacé template no. 2. Stick the picture onto the card and raise it into a 3D picture according to the cutting instructions. Draw a yellow or blue decorative line around the card 0.25 cm from the edge.

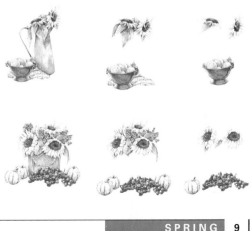

4.

Wedding

An excellent opportunity
to send an attractive
card.

What you need:
- ❏ Lacé templates no. 2, 4, 5 and 8
- ❏ Gold/ecru duo-colour paper
- ❏ Gold beads
- ❏ 3D cut-out sheets: 3D 357 and
  AV 9333 (Valentine)
- ❏ Double-sided sticky film
- ❏ Edge punch

Make the Lacé border as described in Techniques.

1. Rings
Double card (10.5 x 14.8 cm). Lacé template no. 5.
Stick the 3D picture inside the Lacé border and
the flowers in the corners. Punch out the
bottom and top edges. Cut out a circle (Ø 10 cm)
from the duo-colour paper and cut a hole
(Ø 8.5 cm) in this circle to make a ring. Stick this
ring around the Lacé border.

2. Bridal bouquet
Double card (14 x 14 cm). Lacé template no. 8.
Stick a piece of card onto the double-sided
sticky film. Cut four 0.5 cm wide strips from this
and stick these onto the card. Stick a 3D picture
inside the Lacé border and a small heart from
the cut-out sheet in each corner.

3. Love letter
Double card (10.5 x 11 cm). Lacé template no. 4.
Stick a gold circle (Ø 4 cm) inside the Lacé
border. Stick the 3D picture onto this and stick
small hearts around the Lacé border.

4. Tree
Double card (10.5 x 14.8 cm). Lacé template no. 2.
Sew a gold bead in each corner of the Lacé
border.
Stick a piece of card onto double-sided sticky
film. Cut three 0.5 cm wide strips from this and
stick them lengthways on the right-hand side of
the card. Stick the gold side of the duo-colour
paper on the inside of the card. Finally, stick the
3D picture onto the card.

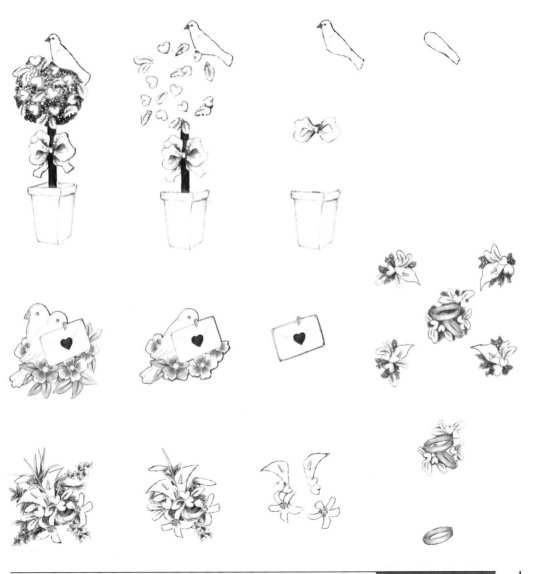

1.

2.

3.

4.

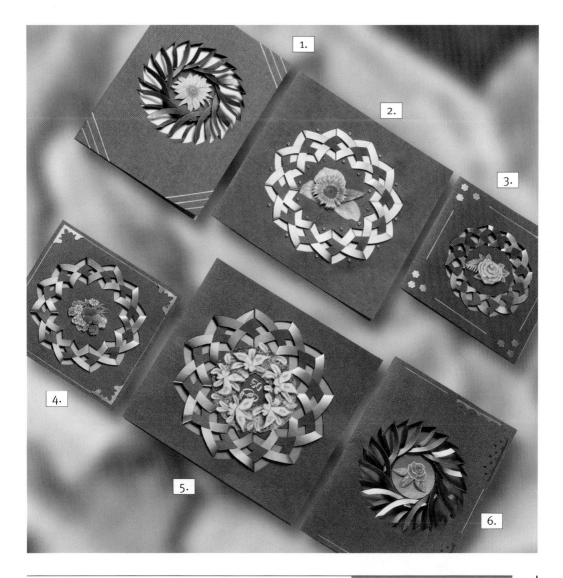

1.
2.
3.
4.
5.
6.

Fun with flowers

This new mother-of-pearl paper is great when combined with flowers.

What you need:
- ❏ *Lacé templates no. 3, 4, 6 and 8*
- ❏ *Brown/gold and green/gold mother-of-pearl duo-colour paper*
- ❏ *Gold beads*
- ❏ *3D pictures of flowers*
- ❏ *Gold gel pen*
- ❏ *Edge ornament punch (by Tom Tas)*

Make the Lacé border as described in Techniques.

1. Rectangular brown card
Double card (10.5 x 14.8 cm). Lacé template no. 6.
Stick the picture inside the Lacé border and draw three lines in the corners using the gel pen.

2. Large brown card
Double card (14 x 14 cm). Lacé template no. 8.
Sew gold beads onto the card. To finish it off nicely, stick coloured paper on the inside of the card. Stick the 3D picture onto the card.

3. Small brown card
Double card (10.5 x 10.5 cm). Lacé template no. 4.
Stick the 3D picture inside the Lacé border. Punch out four flowers and stick these in each corner of the card. Finally, draw gold decorative lines between the flowers.

4. Small green card
Double card (10 x 10 cm). Lacé template no. 3.
Punch out four gold corner pieces and stick these in each corner of the card. Draw decorative gold lines from corner to corner and stick the 3D picture onto the card using glue.

5. Large green card
Double card (14 x 14 cm). Lacé template no. 8.
Stick the 3D picture onto the card. In the middle of this, stick a sticker with, for example, the number 50.

6. Rectangular green card
Double card (10.5 x 14.8 cm). Lacé template no. 6.

Cut out a circle (Ø 3 cm) out of the gold paper and stick this inside the Lacé border. Stick the picture onto this using the 3D glue. Punch out an edge in the top and bottom right-hand corners and connect these punch patterns by drawing gold lines.

Birth

Purple and pink or blue and yellow combine very nicely for baby cards.

What you need:
- ❏ Lacé templates no. 2, 3, 7 and 8
- ❏ Blue/yellow and purple/ pink duo-colour paper
- ❏ Corner punch
- ❏ Embossing stencil EC 9722 (by Avec)
- ❏ Alphabet stencil
- ❏ Happy Papers baby motives (by Kars)
- ❏ Eyelet and eyelet punch
- ❏ Text sticker, gel pens

Make the Lacé border as described in Techniques.

1. Pink card
Purple/pink duo-colour paper (14.8 x 10.5 cm). Lacé template no. 3. Stick the picture inside the Lacé border and raise it into a 3D picture. Draw blue decorative lines and write the text using the alphabet stencil.

2. Label
Purple/pink duo-colour paper (7.2 x 10 cm). Lacé template no. 2. Cut out the picture. Raise it into a 3D picture and stick it in the bottom right-hand corner using 3D glue . Draw a purple decorative line around the card 0.25 cm from the edge. Write text using the embossing stencil. Punch an eyelet in the top left-hand corner and tie a ribbon through it.

3. Purple card
Purple/pink duo-colour paper (14 x 14 cm). Lacé template no. 7. Stick the picture inside the Lacé border. Punch out four corner pieces and stick these onto a pink decorative line. Finally, stick a text sticker onto the card.

4. Blue card
Blue/yellow duo-colour paper (14.5 x 14.5 cm). Lacé template no. 8. For instructions, see card 3, except write the text with a yellow gel pen.

5. Yellow card
Blue/yellow duo-colour paper (14.8 x 10.5 cm). Lacé template no. 2. Stick the picture in the bottom right-hand corner. Write a blue text.

Autumn

The colours of this duo-colour paper in combination with the pictures make attractive autumn cards.

What you need:
- ❏ Lacé templates no. 3 and 5
- ❏ Brown/green duo-colour paper
- ❏ Silver origami paper
- ❏ Ornare pricker and pricking stencil
- ❏ Brown beads and glass beads
- ❏ Shake-it cut-out sheet IT 322
- ❏ Adhesive butterfly pictures
- ❏ Squirrel cut-out sheet
- ❏ Eyelet and eyelet punch
- ❏ Ecru cord
- ❏ Foam tape

Make the Lacé border as described in Techniques.

1. Card with a brown circle
Double card (10.5 x 14.8 cm). Lacé template no. 3.
Stick silver origami paper to the back of the Lacé border. Stick a piece of duo-colour paper to the inside of the card to make it look nice. Cut out a circle (Ø 10 cm) and cut a hole (Ø 7.5 cm) in this to make a ring. Prick holes around the edge of the ring as you wish using the Ornare pricker and sew beads onto the ring. Curl the edges of the pictures to give a raised effect and stick them onto the card with 3D glue.

2. Card with pricked edge
Double card (11.5 x 14.8 cm). Lacé template no. 5.
Prick a decorative edge around the card using the Ornare pricking stencil. Stick the butterfly inside the Lacé border. Fold the wings upwards and place 3D glue under them.

3. Card with a squirrel

Double card (14 x 14 cm). Lacé template no. 5.
Cut out a circle (Ø 12 cm) and cut a hole
(Ø 8.5 cm) in this circle to make a ring. Use the
hole punch to make 16 holes in the ring. Punch
the eyelets into these holes using an eyelet
punch or a Prym tool. Next, thread a thin ecru
cord through the holes. Stick the ring onto the
card using foam tape. Stick the picture inside
the Lacé border and raise it into a 3D picture.

4. Green circle with beads

*Double card (14 x 14 cm). Lacé template no. 3.
Silver origami paper (13.2 x 13.2 cm). Brown/
green duo-colour paper (13 x 13 cm).*
Cut out a circle (Ø 11.8 cm) and cut a hole
(Ø 9.4 cm) in this circle to make a ring. Prick a

pattern onto the ring using an Ornare pricking
stencil and sew beads onto the ring. Next, stick
the ring onto the brown card. Fold the autumn
leaf near the veins, so that it looks like a real
leaf and stick it onto the card using 3D glue.

5. Card with a square frame

Double card (13 x 13 cm). Lacé template no. 5.
Cut a 1.5 cm wide frame (11.5 x 11.5 cm) out of
the brown duo-colour paper. Use the hole
punch to make sixteen holes in the frame. Next,
stick eyelets in the holes using an eyelet punch
or a Prym tool and then thread a thin ecru cord
through the holes. Stick the frame onto the card
using foam tape. Finally, stick the butterfly in
the middle of the card. Fold the wings upwards
and stick 3D glue under them.

Birth cutting instructions

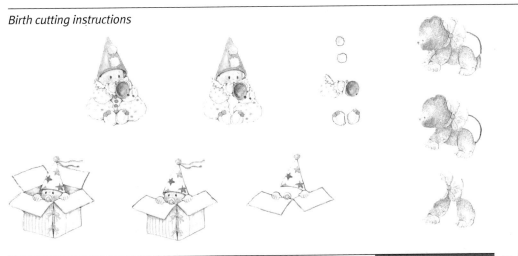

1.

2.

3.

4.

5.

Christmas

Attractive round

Lacé borders for

festive cards.

What you need:
- ❏ Lacé templates no. 3, 4 and 5
- ❏ Red/green duo-colour paper
- ❏ Card: Red, dark green and black
- ❏ Red and gold origami paper
- ❏ Angel punch and round edge punch
- ❏ 3D cut-out sheets 3D 363
- ❏ Shake-it cut-out sheets:
     IT 325, IT 326 and IT 337
- ❏ Gold ribbon
- ❏ Eyelets and eyelet punch
- ❏ Gel pen
- ❏ Adhesive stars
- ❏ Gold stamp-pad ink

Make the Lacé border as described in Techniques.

1. Red card with stripy corners
Double card (10.5 x 14.8 cm). Lacé template no. 4.

Stick gold origami paper to the inside of the card. Stick gold origami paper onto double-sided sticky film and cut 2 mm wide strips from this. Stick these strips in all four corners of the card.
Stick a Christmas star inside the Lacé border using 3D glue. Make a bow from gold ribbon and stick this onto the card with the ribbon under the star.

2. Green card with a punched out circle
Double card (14 x 14 cm). Lacé template no. 4.
Punch out the red border with angels according to the punch pattern on page 24 and stick this onto a circle (Ø 12.5 cm) made from gold origami paper. Cut out a circle (Ø 8 cm) from the green/red paper and make the Lacé border on the green side. Stick this circle onto the gold origami paper circle (Ø 8.5 cm) and stick a small Christmas decoration inside the Lacé border using 3D glue.

3. Red card with springs of holly
Double black card (10.5 x 14.8 cm). Red card (9.5 x 14 cm) with gold origami paper or holographic paper stuck to the back of it. Lacé template no. 3.
Stick the stars and the 3D picture onto the card.

4. Red card with a small house

Double red card (13 x 13 cm). Green card
(12 x 12 cm) with silver origami paper
stuck to the back of it. Lacé
template no. 5.
Punch out the corners of the
green card. Make a hole and
punch an eyelet through it.
Stick the red ribbon under
the picture and to the rear
of the card. Stick the
house in the middle of the
Lacé border using 3D glue.
Draw a decorative line
around the card 0.5 cm from
the edge. Stick stars in the
corners.

5. Red card with a Christmas ball

Red card (13 x 13 cm). Black card
(12 x 12 cm) with gold origami paper stuck to
the back of it. Lacé template no. 3.
For instructions, see card no. 4.

6. Green card with strips

For instructions, see card no. 1, expect do not
include the gold circle (Ø 8.5 cm).

7. Red card with punched out circle

For instructions, see card no. 2, except use
different colours and a different picture.

Punch pattern: Angels

1.

2.

3.

4.

5.

Get well soon

What you need:
- ❏ *Lacé templates no. 1, 2, 3 and 4*
- ❏ *Card: Purple, black and white*
- ❏ *Silver origami paper*
- ❏ *Text stickers*
- ❏ *Glass beads*
- ❏ *Condolence illustrations*

Make the Lacé border as described in Techniques.

1. Square card
Purple double card (11.5 x 11.5 cm). Black circle (Ø 10 cm) with silver origami paper stuck to the back of it. Lacé template no. 3. Draw a silver decorative line around the card 0.5 cm from the edge. Stick a text sticker inside the Lacé border.

2. White rectangular card
White double card (10.5 x 13.8 cm). Two strips of black card (3.3 x 13.8 cm) Lacé template no. 1. Stick a text sticker and the 3D picture onto the black strip on the right-hand side.

3. Black card
Black double card (10.5 x 14.8 cm). Black/ white duo-colour paper. Lacé template no. 4. Cut the Lacé pattern on the white side of the duo-colour paper and then make the pattern 0.5 cm larger. Prick holes in the corners and sew glass beads to them. Stick the 3D picture in the middle of the Lacé border. Stick an extra piece of paper on the inside of the card to hide the thread. Stick a suitable text sticker onto the card and draw decorative lines using the gel pen.

4. White card
White double card (10.5 x 14.8 cm). Black/white duo-colour paper. Lacé template no. 3. For instructions, see card no. 3.

5. Purple card
Purple double card (10.5 x 13.8 cm). Two strips of black card (3.3 x 13.8 cm); stick silver origami paper to one of the strips. Lacé template no. 1. For instructions, see card no. 1.

Glossy denim

Attractive glossy blue denim cards. This paper is also suitable for matching envelopes.

What you need:
- ❏ *Lacé templates no. 3, 5, 6 and 7*
- ❏ *Blue/silver duo-colour paper*
- ❏ *White and silver gel pens*
- ❏ *Silver beads*
- ❏ *3D flower pictures*

Make the Lacé border as described in Techniques.

Matching envelopes can be made as shown by the diagrams on page 31.

1. Large square card
Double card (14 x 14 cm). Lacé template no. 7.
Stick the 3D picture inside the Lacé border. Draw a silver decorative line around the card 0.8 cm from the edge.

2. Rectangular card with stripes
Double card (10.5 x 14.8 cm). Lacé template no. 6.
Cut out a silver circle (Ø 3.3 cm) and stick this in the centre of the Lacé border. Stick the 3D picture onto this circle using 3D glue. Stick a piece of duo-colour paper onto double-sided sticky film and cut 0.5 cm wide strips from this. Stick these strips in the corners of the card.

3. Rectangular card with beads
Double card (10.5 x 14.8 cm). Lacé template no. 3.
Stick the 3D picture onto the card and sew silver beads around the edge of the Lacé border.

4. Small card
Double card (10.5 x 10.5 cm). Lacé template no. 5.
Stick the 3D picture in the middle of the Lacé border and draw a white line around the card 0.5 cm from the edge and colour the corners.

1.

2.

3.

4.

1.

2.

3.

4.

5.

Prettige Feestdagen

More Christmas

You can also make attractive Christmas cards using these colours.

What you need:
- ❏ Lacé templates no. 3, 4 and 7
- ❏ Black/white duo-colour paper
- ❏ Red and gold origami paper
- ❏ Ornare pricking stencil
- ❏ Holly punch
- ❏ Red glass beads and gold beads
- ❏ Eyelets and eyelet punch
- ❏ Embossing stencil EC9725 (by Avec)
- ❏ 3D cut-out sheets:
  3D 364, 3D 371 and 3D 353

Make the Lacé border as described in Techniques.

1. White card
Double card (14 x 14 cm). Lacé template no. 7. Use an Ornare pricking stencil to make a decorative edge and sew red glass beads onto the holes. Stick the 3D picture in the middle of the card. Cut out the two apples. Stick the right-hand and then the left-hand apple onto the card using 3D glue. Finish the card off by sticking red origami paper to the inside of the card.

2. Merry Christmas
Double card (10.5 x 14.8 cm). Gold card (10 x 13.8 cm). Single black card (9.5 x 13.3 cm). Lacé template no. 4. Sew gold beads around the Lacé border and stick the 3D picture in the middle. Use an embossing stencil to write the gold text.

3. Black card with lace dressing
Double card (13.5 x 13.5 cm). Lacé template no. 3. Cut out a white circle (Ø 12.5 cm). Use the holly punch and copy the pattern shown on page 32. Cut out a black circle (Ø 9 cm) and stick this inside the white circle. Stick a circle (Ø 8.5 cm) made from red origami paper on the back of the Lacé border. Stick the picture in the middle of the card using 3D glue.

4. Black card
Double card (14.5 x 14.5 cm). Lacé template no. 7. Sew red glass bead onto the points of the Lacé pattern. Stick a small Christmas tree ball onto the card using 3D glue. Make a hole above the Lacé border and pinch an eyelet in this. Thread

a gold ribbon through the eyelet and stick this under the ball and to the rear of the card. Stick gold origami paper against the inside of the card. Use a gold gel pen to draw a decorative line around the card 1 cm from the edge.

5. White card with lace dressing

For instructions, see card no. 3, except use different colours and a different picture.

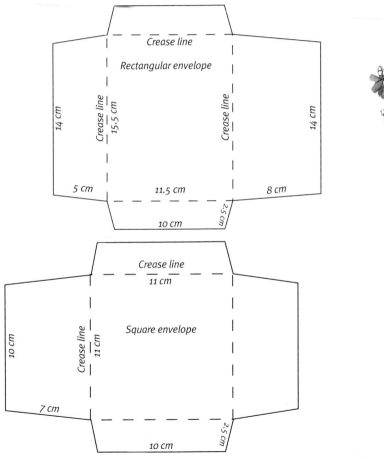

Crease line

Rectangular envelope

Crease line

Crease line

14 cm

Crease line

15.5 cm

14 cm

5 cm

11.5 cm

8 cm

2.5 cm

10 cm

Crease line

11 cm

10 cm

Crease line

11 cm

Square envelope

7 cm

2.5 cm

10 cm

Punch pattern: Holly

Special thanks to:
Kars & Co. B.V., Ochten, the Netherlands, for the use of the materials.